Sac
Sutı

Radical Insights On Sex, Love, Tantra, Kink & Other Spiritual Pursuits

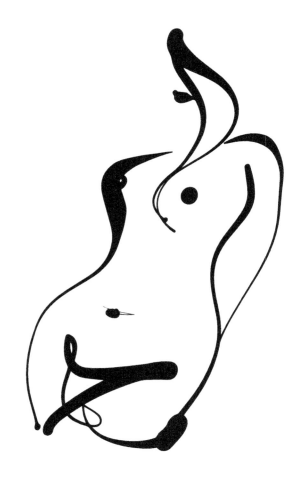

Kamala Devi
Art by François Dubeau

Published by

ZENDOW PRESS

ISBN: 10-0-9896485-6-7
ISBN: 13-978-0-9896485-6-1

Published by Zendow Press.
San Diego, California, USA

Library of Congress Cataloging-in-Publication Data
First edition copyright © 2016 KamalaDevi McClure

All the art in this collection is reproduced with full permission from
Prose Inc. Copyright retained by François Dubeau.
www.FrancoisDubeau.com

"Ecosex Sutras" were first published in *ECOSEXUALITY*:
When Nature Inspires the Arts of Love © 2015 by Serena
Anderlini-D'Onofrio and Lindsay Hagamen with 3WayKiss. Copyright
retained by Kamala Devi. www.KamalaDevi.com

To My Beloved Michael

There is no temple, no book nor teacher –of love–
that is more revelatory to me than you. Our dance is
a perfectly-tailored curriculum that forces my heart
into quantum expansion. You are my lord, my
liberator, and the greatest love of my life.

Praise for

Sacred Slut
Sutras

It's damn good. The aphoristic approach gives one something to mull over in meditation. It is a book that people will pick up time and again in the midst of a lively conversation. I've taken four initiations in Tibetan Tantra, so the concepts are close to my heart. This book is dynamite and I'm delighted to have read it!

–Tim Fullerton
Published Poet and Ordained Buddhist Priest for over 40 years

Everything Kamala Devi touches turns to Gold. She has created are markable offering of poetry for Lovers! Allow her to touch you with her Sutras.

–Caroline Muir
Author *Tantra Goddess & Tantra: The Art of Conscious Loving*

If you want something sexy, something different from anything you've ever shared with yourself and your beloved before, you want to read this book. And you want to allow yourself to be taken over by her raw, erotic, fun-loving expression. Truly a gift of love!

–Laurie Handlers
Author of *Sex & Happiness*, Talk Show Host and Filmmaker

Kamala Devi is true, honest, authentic and real. Yes, she is also sexy, eroticly intelligent and a yogini filled with a love for life. She knows by her own direct experience how "sex opens us to the mystery beyond the material." In this book she empties herself into you with love, truth, humour and lust.

–Yoah Wexler
Author of *Knowing Yourself*

These sutras are Rumi on steroids. They are verbal mandalas, many with the capacity for profound transformation, simply by the reader taking in their message. In another age, they would be burned for their power. I had to stop and weep...then laugh, then sob...multiple times. A number of times, they bored fissures so deep into the nature of things, and revealed new and wild, yet intimately familiar, species of attitudes, emotions, and truths. I think anyone not shaken to their core by some of these must be asleep.

–Jill Nagle
Author of *Whores and Other Feminists*

Elegant, poetic, visionary, and radical. As always, Kamala Devi brings the purity of her unique voice and vibrant expression to her work. Holding the sacred while fully acknowledging the messy business of being human, "The Sacred Slut Sutras" reorient the seeker should they drift too far in either direction, providing a map to hold both aspects and to allow them to dance together.

–Katie Weatherup
Author of *Practical Shamanism, A Guide for Walking in Both Worlds*

The Sacred Slut Sutras will have you more connected to the ever overflowing truth of your own being after you've read them alone orwith a friend or lover. They'll make you laugh, cry and moan withdelight.

–Alexis Neely AKA Ali Shanti
Author of *Wear Clean Underwear*, Entrepreneur & Mother

Kamala Devi delivers truth in tiny, but potent and juicy, packages! Don't read these sutras unless you are ready to dance with your deepest core and get cracked wide open. Better yet, read them to your lover and savor them one luscious bite at a time.

–Amrita Grace
Award-winning Author of *Reclaiming Aphrodite*

Beware: this slut IS sacred! Allow her to seduce you into Satori. If classic Zen masters spoke of Sex as freely as they spoke of awakening this book would not have been such a novelty.

–Rabbi Ohad Ezrahi
Author of *Kdesha* & 5 more books

Table of Consciousness

Introduction

*I met Rumi by the riverside,
and told him if his pen ever ran
dry, he could dip into my inkwell.
I've been overflowing ever since.*

At first, these deep and dirty lines appeared like distractions from my daily practice of meditation, movement or making love. They were thorns that somehow got stuck between the webs of my fingers. I tried to shake them off, but the poking persisted.

Upon closer inspection, I saw they were pointed little crystals. I plucked them out and passed them around on social media. I was not prepared for the explosive controversy that resulted.

Like-minded readers found these simple aphorisms liberated them from their limitations. But there were others who attacked me publicly, un-friended me and even went as far as writing personal hate mail. Why do these little lines catalyze such fierce love/hate reactions?

We've been fed fear on everything to do with sex. The otherworldliness of orgasm has been suppressed. Spirituality has been relegated to churches and cults. Love's been commodified and sex overregulated. As a result, we're numb to life itself. The truth is…

Sex opens us to the mystery beyond the material.

These sutras disrupt our current constructs in order to unlock a direct channel to the innermost chamber of the body temple. If you've examined conventional taboos and are on a path towards sexual liberation, these lines will quench your thirst. However, if you have not questioned your socially-inflicted sex shame, be warned, this collection may bring up bile.

The scope of these sutras do not stop at sacred sexuality. Tantra is an exploration of all of existence. The consciousness that makes me and you is the same animating force that moves through everything. As such these are meditations on death, travel, work, writing, mother nature and more!

Ultimately, by sharing the unique way the Universe moves through me, I hope to give you permission to express your perspective, way beyond any cultural limitations on love!

I sometimes write statements in first person, to hold up a mirror. Other times, I'll make sweeping generalizations in third person. I may even offer unsolicited advice. Whether the insight is universal or idiosyncratic, I hope you take pleasure in these edgy, profound, sexy, sarcastic and sometimes even silly sutras. Indulge.

Wake Up and Dream,

KamalaDevi

Agape

*Loving you is like
being sentenced to liberation.*

I feel you so deeply
inside me that making
love is redundant.

Love may be blind from the
outside, but it opens an inner
vision to the absolute.

"What is the taste of love?"
I ask and the beloved answers:
"It tastes of air, it is ever
present."

Agape

You have touched my being so
thoroughly that I no
longer recognize myself as
separate from you.

My heart is under renovation;
the entrance was once an
obstacle course, but now I'm
building a landing strip.

It's no longer a surprise that
I can fall deeply, truly, madly in
LOVE in just one night —
I just wonder why I don't
do it every day.

I used to dream of expanding my container in order to experience more love but when I woke up, I realized love need not be contained.

Unconditional love is ever present and life-giving like the sun. Our human capacity is but a partial reflection that waxes and wanes more like the moon.

Agape

Our love is bigger than the fluctuations of mood, mind or even the balance of your bank account. After the storm passes and the clouds of your current circumstances clear, my heart will still be ablaze for you.

Art

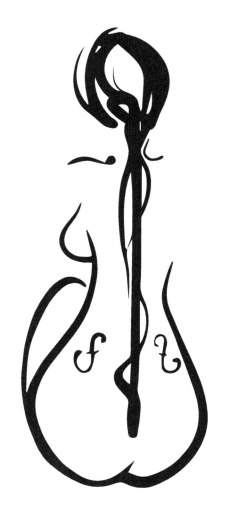

*My creative inspiration is so
intertwined with my sexual
arousal, it's a shame
to untangle them.*

To ensure the creativity never runs dry, I am constantly pumping the source.

⌒ℓ

I am an artist. My medium is love. And like most eccentric creatives, my art is misunderstood.

⌒ℓ

I've met many muses in my life; rare and precious are the ones who keep a calendar and get shit done.

Art

There's a thin line between art
and therapy; I'm never sure
from moment to moment
which side I'm on.

～ら

The experiences that are worth
framing are the ones that go
beyond any frame of reference
I've ever known.

～ら

My art oscillates between
periods of narcissistic self
indulgence and courageous
service to the collective.

I dreamt I was driving an RV and to get better wifi reception, I decided to park at the intersection between Art and Porn.

~⌣~

Creativity moves like the ocean. Retreating to gather inspiration before surging forth with another powerful manifestation.

~⌣~

Sometimes it's so bad we have to scrap our inspiration and start over from scratch. Other times it's perfect without any revision. Usually it's somewhere in between.

Art

*The muse can be cruel.
She starts by nibbling on my
earlobe; if that doesn't inspire
me, she bites; and if I ignore
her, she's been known to shoot
her venom into my veins.*

～

*If you like my style —don't copy
me — copy my authenticity.*

～

*A true muse doesn't just
leave the artist pregnant with
inspiration, but shows them
how to breathe through
delivery and fortifies them
with the gumption to raise
the damn thing.*

*I create art on behalf
of the collective. My art
is for all the sexual outcasts,
perverts and pioneers who
were branded as witches
and devil worshipers. My
art is for my ancestors,
as well as generations
to come.*

Art

If the artist isn't careful, the subject might spill off the canvas and accidentally color the artist's life.

Breathing

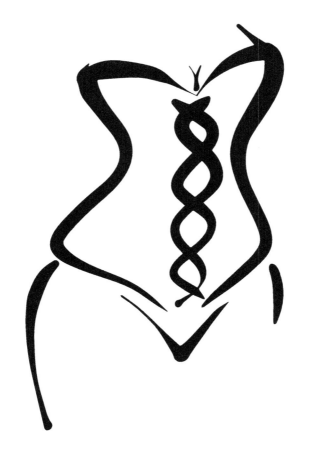

*To find immortality, you need
not drink another's blood, or
die to the daylight — instead
sip from radiance between
each breath — that is the real
juice of the human heart.*

If you carefully escort each breath out on the exhale, it cannot abandon you.

〜

I lost myself somewhere between the inhalation and the exhalation; now the finding is ceaseless. Loving is like breathing.

〜

Societal restrictions that dictate who and how we love pollute the atmosphere and pinch off our air supply.

Breathing

Breathing is a metaphor for love. Though we constantly forget to do it, it continues to move through us. Even when we are unaware, it is the very force that keeps us alive.

Within every person, in every moment, magic unfolds if we notice how the fullness of breath naturally flips inside out — becoming empty again — until the end of our existence.

Love in. Love out. I receive love on the inhalation and release love on the exhalation. I just can't be held accountable for what happens during those damn retentions.

Breathing

Though we constantly forget to appreciate it, the breathing is happening anyway. Once aware of it, we have a choice whether or not to meet it with our sensuality.

Compassion

Compassion is that place where the heart turns inside out, and meets itself again.

Staying bitter is lazy,
compared to the deep and
humbling work
of forgiveness.

～

Empathy doesn't come by just
looking into someone's eyes,
but looking through them.

～

When surfing in the sea of
compassion, the trick is not
to wipe-out in a wave of co-
dependence.

Compassion

The trouble with being a transpersonal channel is that you love with all the hearts that ever loved, but you also hurt that way.

Compassion comes with knowing that reality is always perceived and projected through our own partial perspectives.

If my heart is ripping clear down the center and I come to you for help, sometimes the most compassionate response is to brandish a meat cleaver.

We cannot become whole in ourselves unless we strive to see the wholeness in others.

Compassion

Criticism forms a wall between me and humanity. When I drop the judgement, a secret door opens so I can re-enter a state of grace.

Death

I'm finally starting to appreciate the wisdom of the long lingering good-bye. It's what we've all been doing since our arrival here on Earth. Why rush it?

I know death is on my dance card but I am not chasing after it, nor running away.

~

Waking up is dying to the unreal.

~

Time is my most sacred possession, and like everything else I "own," it's only borrowed.

Death

To withhold love — for fear of hurt — is as absurd as choosing not to live, because inevitably we all die.

∿

There is something sick about a society that insists on putting hairspray and makeup on the deceased.

∿

There is nothing to fear, if death is anything like sleep. However if we must first pass through a bardo, made up of mind, our cultural panic may be justified.

Tonight I die to the past and pray she passes swiftly. God help me push my unwanted history off a volcanic ridge and watch her be instantly incinerated rather than suffer as my spent days slowly freeze in the gradual stages of hypothermia.

Death

Our eternal essence is too expansive for this temporary and partial perspective.

Ecosexuality

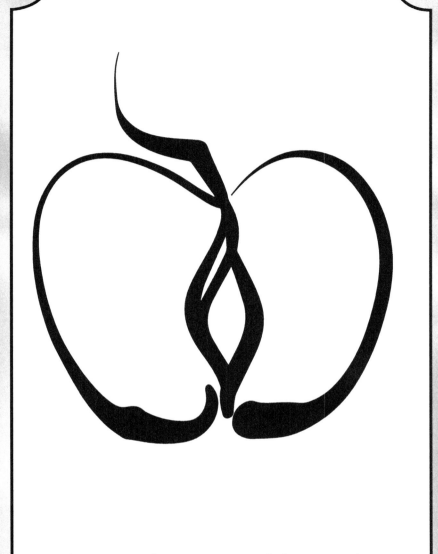

I started a vegetable garden just so that I could grow my own organic dildos.

I want to wrap my legs
around the world.

⁓

You know you're ecosexual
when you get splinters
on your tongue.

⁓

Bananas are perfectly shaped,
but too soft for women with
strong kegel muscles.

Ecosexuality

Sunbathing is so sensual, but my sunburn is not sexy, like an ecosex shame hangover.

~

Spring: A curious season in which I compulsively look out windows to see what is emerging.

~

How can I be satisfied by the beauty of the ocean's surface when she keeps calling me into her depths?

Earth mamma brings me flowers, she bears me fruit, she massages my feet, and holds me tirelessly in her arms of gravity.

~

We've covered her skin with concrete, pumped her full of plastic, bulldozed down her pulmonary branches and are selling her blood for over $3 a gallon.

Ecosexuality

As I run my hands down to the base of her trunk, I feel for the soft ticklish places that peek out between bits of bark, until I get to that vulnerable spot where she splits into roots and merges into Earth.

In the beginning, night fell on top of daylight and made such passionate love that colors soaked the sky. Twilight was so good that they agreed to do it again, every day, at sunrise and sunset, for eternity.

*When the wilderness wants
to be watched, it's not from
behind a window.*

Ecosexuality

Small-minded people who can't handle the progressive beauty of mixed-species love often use "tree-hugger" as a derogatory term.

Eros

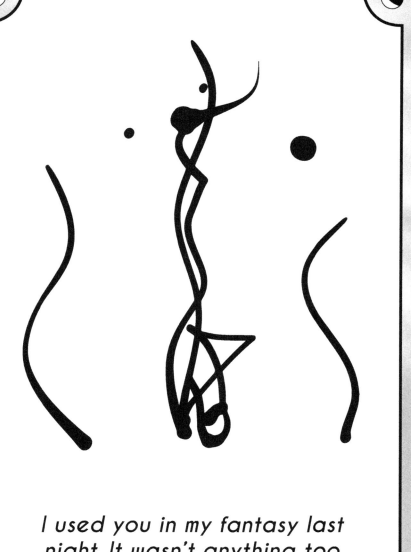

I used you in my fantasy last night. It wasn't anything too elaborate or perverted, but it will forever change the way I think of you.

*I yearn to violate you
with my love.*

~

*I love the little show I get
when you accidentally drop
something and have to bend
over to pick it up.*

~

*If you open my heart, my legs
will naturally want to follow.*

Eros

A slow seduction is underway;
regardless of who started it,
the imperative is to surrender.

Make love to the whole before
penetrating the hole.

You activate my wetness ...
and the tears that flow in your
presence are so much sweeter
than the tears stimulated
by sorrow.

*Your touch instantly
accelerates my heartbeat; but
a strategically-placed kiss
can suspend me to something
slower than a stop.*

*When I touch myself, it's not
so much that I think of you,
but that I think — I am you —
touching me, all curious and
eager about my femininity.*

Eros

It's natural for my vagina to get sore after a long night of sex, but how about the heart? Have you ever felt bruised and achy from loving so much?

Goddess Worship

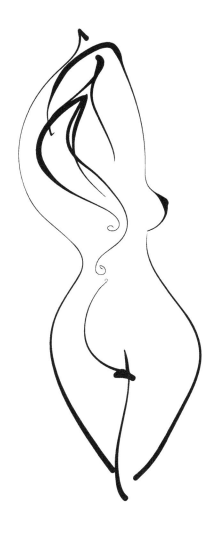

Regardless of whether you believe in God, the Goddess works through me.

Her essence is too expansive
for my partial perspective.

⁓

Yoni. Pussy. Vagina. Cunt:
A rose is a rose is a rose
is a rose.

⁓

I prayed for the Goddess
to speak through me.
Then I lost my voice.

Goddess Worship

I want to love as God loves. But when I fall short, I blame it on having internal genitalia.

～

When I close my eyes, I see God; when I open my eyes, she's still there — just in disguise.

～

Once in a while I catch a glimpse of the shadow side of the Goddess within, and she scares the shit out of me.

God is boundless, yes, but she is also found within the boundaries and honored in the act of setting them.

~

Woman thou art profane, prostitute, wench, whore, harlot, slut, tramp, Jezebel, floozy, hooker, hussy, nymphomaniac, streetwalker, strumpet, tramp, trollop, bitch.

~

Woman thou art sacred, Goddess, priestess, prophetess, muse, angel, divine, pure, revered, saintly, sanctified, venerable mother, creator.

Goddess Worship

On this day, I die to the past, forgive everything, and pray for the Goddess to be re-born in my body. Damn, I always forget to specify, "gently, please Goddess, take me gently.

It's not enough to know God, I must also make her my consort.

Gratitude

Thank everyone who's ever helped me as well as anyone who's ever hurt me.

Entitlement is the enemy
of Gratitude.

⌒

I'm drenched in gratitude,
daily, for the gift of this body.

⌒

I cannot be bothered by lack,
when I am far too fascinated
by the mysterious way life
has of filling it.

Gratitude

In opening my awareness to all
that is deserving of gratitude,
I realize how much I'm still
taking for granted.

Gratitude is simply a side effect
of consciousness. The more I
wake up, the more I become
aware of life's boundless
blessings.

Gratitude can be used like a baby's pacifier: when the heart compulsively reaches for something that's missing, simply stuff a "thank you" in its place.

Gratitude

*If I remembered to practice
gratitude on every breath
since the day I was born, I'd
still have more blessings
than I could count.*

Heartache

I don't know why I'm crying.
The mind may make up a story,
but these tears come straight
from the heart.

Our love was once otherworldly, now we're worlds apart.

~

My heart bursts into shrapnels, in service to Cupid, who needs frequent target practice.

~

I think of you with the same compulsion that leads a criminal back to the scene of the crime.

Heartache

My heart feels as useless as the husk of a cocoon after its inhabitants have hatched and flown away.

Getting over you is like telling my tongue to stop feeling around for the tooth that used to be there.

Love hurts. Love encompasses the full range of human condition. And suffering is a part of the human experience.

My heart aches not from the loss or lack of your love, but from having held back my own.

~

I miss you. More accurately, I miss the idea of you. But at least I've got a lively dialogue going with a more available version of you, in my mind.

Heartache

It still hurts so bad, because our love went all the way down to the core, and now it seems that the love is gone but the wound is still there. Yet, in ultimate reality, it's the other way around.

Humor

*Your inappropriate humor
makes me want to
spread my legs.*

Cogito ertic sum: I fuck therefore I am.

I am not schizophrenic but my vaginas are.

My boyfriend measures his excitement in inches.

Humor

If you are not pissing off the pope, you are not playing hard enough.

When my chiropractor heard that my neck injury came from oral sex, he gave me a high five.

Before enlightenment: chop wood, carry water. After tantric enlightenment: sport wood, squirt water.

Ninjas sometimes pretend to meditate, when really, they are invading other people's meditations.

~

Tantra can't be taught in words. If you're going to read about it, the book should at least have pictures.

~

If infinite intelligence came down to Earth and took the form of a woman, I'd challenge her to a naked oil wrestling match.

Humor

*If you meet the Buddha
on the road, fuck him.*

Kink

*In consensual fantasy play,
shameful memories can earn
triumphant new endings.*

Whenever I start to feel a little weird, I go to a public dungeon with a bunch of perverts and walk away feeling rather normal.

~

The prime directive is to do no harm; but in the name of pleasure, a little pain is justifiable.

~

Compared to who I am in my fantasies, I am a very good girl; so glad dreamtime knows no consequence.

Kink

I'm disoriented by this upside-down society and often can't tell top from bottom. But at least in the bedroom, I know my place.

～～

There is a shape-shifting, time-traveling, fantasy-fulfilling field of permission that is born by our consensual perversion.

～～

"Trust, boundaries, breathwork and presence" — are we talking about BDSM or Tantra? Regardless, when practiced in earnest, both paths lead to ultimate surrender.

I cultivate a passionate mystique by never speaking of my perverted fantasies. This practice does not, however, stop me from occasionally hinting, or playing them out.

~

Power exchange cuts across all kinds of disciplines. Dominance and submission shows up as butch/femme in queer culture, guru/disciple in yoga, Shiva/ Shaktiin Tantra, and in kink it's boils down to top and bottom.

Kink

I daydream about a strong tantric dominatrix bending me over her knee and demanding: "Who's your deity?"

Life

I'm on one hell of a roller coaster ride, but so is everyone else who is alive.

Whether you embrace it or not, evolution has its arms around us. Since one-way hugs are awkward, you might as well hug back.

~

Reality is squishy, isn't it?

~

No matter how seductive the show, please don't let me forget that I am the main author, actor and audience of my life.

Life

Evolution is unfolding through us. Our work is to keep opening to it.

～

I don't believe in Miracles, I live one.

～

Personal growth is like fitness, we don't finish a great workout and then never need to exercise again. The day we stop working on ourselves is the day we start dying.

Somewhere along the path,
I walked into a labyrinth.
Today, without ceremony, the
way in simply turned into the
way out. The solution is simple:
add one part problem, to two
parts possibility and allow it to
dissolve into acceptance.

~

We are all weaving this
collective dream; some of us
are a bit more lucid than those
who tend towards nightmares.

Life

Evolution is unstoppable.
Growth may happen in fits
and spurts, and may be stunted
by un-fertile grounds,
or bitter seasons, but evolution
never ceases.

Listening

*Loving is so close to listening
that the difference
often dissolves.*

Every time I stop to listen, there is a constant conversation going on in my body about how I can feel more connection.

~

Thanks for not attaching to anything I say because when I'm truly inspired, my deepest beliefs become outdated upon utterance.

~

Holding space is listening for who you are, regardless of the words and tone and gestures — who are you beyond all that?

Listening

By hearing how somebody lost their way, you are helping them find it.

~~~

If you truly know how to listen, there are angels all around you, singing their hearts out.

~~~

When you don't know what to say, Listen.

Love

When in love, be gentle. You are responsible for holding a precious piece of another's heart in yours.

Love is not what we THINK it is.

~

Deep in my heart I built an altar and lit a candle for you.

~

Though I have been touched by many, my heart is like a diamond and can only be cut by another diamond, like yours.

Love

Knowing when to lean in, and when to back off, makes loving like dancing.

∿

Touched by love, life blossoms into new depth and dimension.

∿

... and then, without notice, a door had opened, in my heart, to a room I never knew existed....

I am at the center of my Universe, just as you are the center of yours; by loving each other, our worlds merge into infinity.

~

If I am to surrender fully to the totality of love, then I must also embrace the part of me that wants to run screaming in the opposite direction.

Love

If you are losing yourself in relationship, you may be blinded not by love, but illusion. For, when the love is real, we find ourselves.

Magic

I can tell the future —
because I make it happen.

There is magic in every moment,
but especially in the ones
where we meet.

~e

What magic is possible, if at
the time of the hunt, instead
of scattering and denying our
craft, we band together and
practice with all of our might?

~e

Miracles happen so often that
I just expect them, or is the
other way around?

Magic

At the beginning of every ritual, I pray to step aside and let myself come through.

⌐⌐

I've never experienced an unanswered prayer, they are just not answered yet, or wildly surpassed.

⌐⌐

Our dreams are but strands in the tapestry of life, and when we wake up, we realize we are the weavers.

In prayer, the words we use hardly matter, but miracles are made by how congruently we align with our potential.

~

There is a certain magic that pervades the space between our bodies ... and for my next act, we're going to make it disappear.

~

It's not that you wake up one day and say "Who's writing this script?" and then re-write the whole story. It's something we must practice a little everyday.

Magic

I gave myself to this fire. I warmed my bare skin by the flames, and burned inside with your prayers. With smoke and ash in my lungs, I release these words to the Universe, knowing it is already done. And so it is.

I am the answer to those prayers, the ones you hold so deep in your heart that you forgot you made.

Masturbation

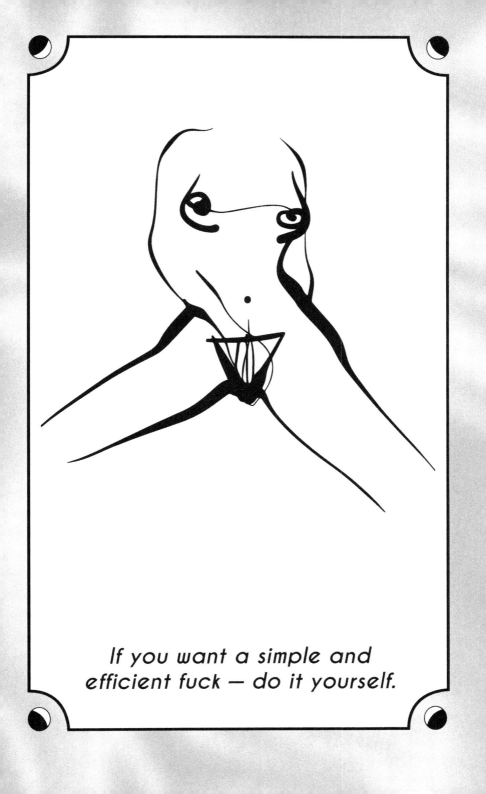

If you want a simple and efficient fuck — do it yourself.

Ode to my handheld
shower head....

～

Masturbation is a moving
meditation.

～

Solo sex need not subtract
from partnered play.

Masturbation

"You again?" My vulva yawns and feigns responsiveness.

If you want extraordinary orgasms, start by taking responsibility for them.

Just had the most profound orgasm ... too bad no one was around to witness it.

Have I gone numb inside or have my fingers finally touched the eye of the storm?

If I don't feel like caressing my breasts, undressing slowly, and adoring my own blossoming body, how can I expect someone else to?

Masturbation

As I plunge into unseen spaces within me, the divine drips down from the base of my skull, tickling the length of my spine on its way to soak the sheets.

Motherhood

*I used to be human, then a
seed was planted inside me, I
swelled with spirit and
life sprang forth.
Now I am a mother.*

Mothering is being an agent of evolution. The directive is to better life, until it grows beyond us.

⌐∿

Motherhood is like joining a cult, or like going codependent because for a period time, you cease being the center of your own Universe.

⌐∿

I never understood the impulse to kill, until after I'd brought life into this world, and something threatened it.

Motherhood

I may know him better, care for him more, and share my whole world with him, but that doesn't make him mine. My son belongs to life itself.

~~~

One of Mommy's innate superpowers is speaking about herself in third person.

~~~

Until your womb has quadrupled in size and an infant rips through your vagina, and your body splits into two ... No, you don't understand.

My relationship to my mother is more complicated than all my other lovers combined. In fact, relating to her makes all other relationships a piece of cake. Thanks Mom.

My womb is a window to the collective. I mourn for the miscarriages, stillbirths, crib deaths and unborn babies of the children I will never have. I celebrate them, too.

Motherhood

The cry of the birthing woman from deep within the womb, beyond the sound of the body stretching open in a hospital bed, is a rally for the millions of Mothers who've been stripped of their sacred station.

Musings

*We live in a garden of
wildflowers, blooming up to
our knees, that sprouted from
seeds that were once
only crazy dreams.*

You don't have to believe your thoughts to trust your intuition.

~

Behold that which activates your arousal and abandon it for nothing.

~

When I feel like I'm losing my mind, I wish I could just call it to listen for the ring.

Musings

Control is thinking I can handle anything; surrender is knowing it can handle itself.

～

Everything is right with the world, except the stuff that is just wrong, and that's all right too.

～

My heart is not just a bird singing from within its cage, or even the cage, but the spaces between the bars.

We may not have any choice about the looks of the face we must wear throughout this lifetime, but from moment to moment, we can choose whether it is smiling or not.

~

Numbness is the saboteur of life. To escape emotion is to shy from existence. When feelings arise,
I amplify them by adding awareness and surfing them back to the source.

Musings

*Stillness in the manifest world
is an illusion. We exist on a
planet that is revolving around
a sun which is also moving.
Thus I center myself in the flow
of my emotions. Who I am is in
constant flux.*

Non
Attachment

Releasing the grasping is not enough. It isn't until we fully open to life that the fixation falls away.

Non attachment is easier to preach than to practice.

∼

Abundance is the reward for releasing attachments.

∼

No matter how much you want it, your happiness does not depend on something being what it is not.

Non Attachment

*How do I not get attached
when my love grows like a vine,
that won't bear fruit or flowers
unless attached.*

~⁀ↄ

*The world is not going to end
if you don't get what you want,
but clinging to the illusion that
you need it might.*

~⁀ↄ

*When my desires become too
intense, a dastardly thing
happens: I confuse them for
needs, and cease enjoying
the pursuit.*

Like thirsty weeds, there are infinite desires overtaking my garden. The dirty dandelion seeds scatter when I sneeze. Zen is simply not in season.

~

I've been attached to being detached and I'm ready to let it all go.

~

To minimize suffering, our culture tells us to increase our having, Buddhism teaches us to decrease our wanting, but I'm busy increasing the satisfaction I feel while longing.

Non Attachment

The renunciation of desire is often a thin mask for the fear of failure. Like children on the playground who have a crush and protect themselves from rejection by projecting cooties onto the opposite sex.

Non-Duality

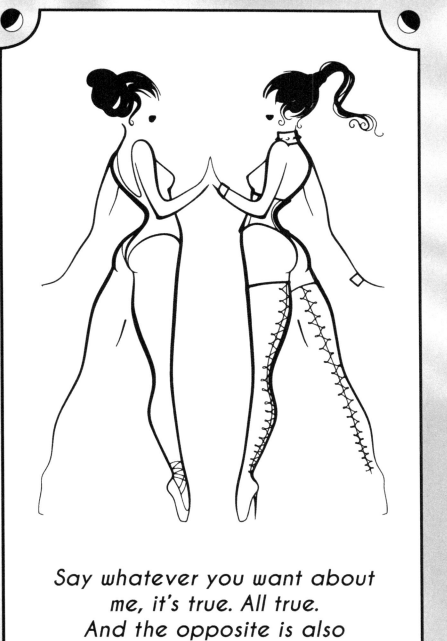

Say whatever you want about
me, it's true. All true.
And the opposite is also
simultaneously true.

I had an elaborate dream
about nothing.

~e

The more dense the matter
the more saturated
with energy it is.

~e

If everything you read seems
to be about you, you're either
egotistical or enlightened.
Or both.

Non-Duality

If you are not willing to cry from the bottom of your heart, how can you expect to love from it?

～

Twilight happens only twice a day — until we expand our awareness and realize it's always happening, somewhere.

～

Just because the interior face of reality does not abide by the same rules as the external objective realm, doesn't make it any less real.

You may see my life and think
that I'm chasing pleasure,
but I assure you, this ecstasy
became sustainable only when
I stopped running away
from pain.

Non-Duality

Where the seeker and the sought become one with this and that; object and subject, I've become.

On Being Human

Most all human challenges
stem from squishing this infinite
unconditional love into limited
mortal flesh and form.

The way to unfeel something is to first feel it.

~

The greatest mistake of the human race is thinking nature is outside.

~

Our defenses dissipate in proportion to the acceptance of our limitation as human beings.

On Being Human

Sleep is the Universe's way of emptying us out at night so that she can fill us each day.

It's humbling and hard to face how human I am when loving you makes me feel immortal.

The mind finds and fixes problems — that's its job — even when there are no problems, it will find one.

I am working overtime to close the dangerous gap between my theory and my practice, before it becomes filled with my apologies.

⌇

Mastery is not a function of having perfected your craft, but of cultivating the necessary skills to swiftly recognize and work on your imperfections.

⌇

My prison walls may be constructed by cognitive misperceptions, but the doorway is clearly made of something beyond mind-stuff.

On Being Human

Intuition is a gift, which, I recently learned the hard way, must be paired with curiosity, lest it turn into assumptions that delude me from reality.

～～

There is an art to making meaning where there is none — AKA — the human experience.

～～

My feelings are but passing clouds driven by the winds of my desires. My true essence is constantly shining underneath like the life-giving sun.

There is a whole sequence
of steps between serving at
the foot of the master, and
dancing around in her shoes,
which involves a great deal of
fumbling around.

On Being Human

Who I am does not stop at the skin, nor merge forever into the formless. I am possibility, taking shape and constantly morphing into creative combinations, furthering the evolution of existence.

Orgasm

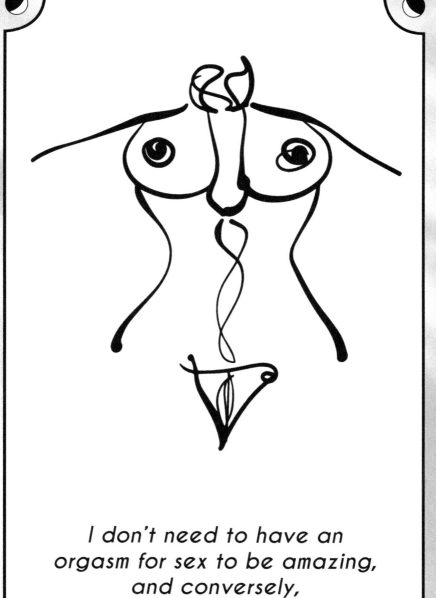

I don't need to have an orgasm for sex to be amazing, and conversely, I don't need sex to have an amazing orgasm!

There are few things that a great orgasm can't solve, or at least that's how it seems for the duration of the climax and however long the afterglow lasts.

~

At point of orgasm, I think of you, every time, no matter who I'm with, I even call out your name.

~

Orgasm is a built-in reminder that great pleasure in life results from both expansions and contractions.

Orgasm

Your orgasm turned me inside out, upside down and, for a few blissful moments, I honestly didn't know how I'd get down from the ceiling.

∾

Being attached to an orgasm is like clinging to the bank of the river that will deliver you.

∾

Having a realization is like having an orgasm — a thrilling and transcendent experience of reality. And my favorite realizations are the ones that come through orgasm!

Perhaps I was too self-conscious, too eager or afraid of peeing on my partners. Whatever the reason was ... it's gone now.

~

Orgasm is a transcendent experience that plugs us into the force that animates all life. We need not wait for specific genital stimulation, just breathe into your connection with the hundreds of thousands of people orgasming right now, throughout the world, and enjoy the ride.

After a long dry journey,
this droplet is returning
to mamma ocean.

Pick-up
lines

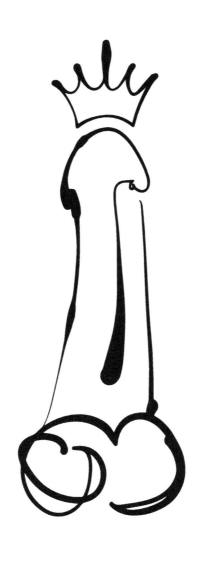

If the Buddha had a wet dream, you'd be it.

You had me at "Namaste."

~⌒

God is Love. Baby,
let's make God tonight.

~⌒

Your body is a temple.
And I want to desecrate it.

Pick-up lines

Your skin smells like home.

～

Your third eye belongs
on my forehead.

～

There is music under your skin,
I can hear it with my tongue.

When I die, I expect the gateway to heaven to look like your inner thighs.

I can't hear the subtle expression of your body language with all those clothes on.

Pick-up lines

Let's connect. Ideally we would make love, but if you're not into it, the next best thing is to fuck. Or just snuggle, or process or even argue. I'll meet you wherever you want,

147

Presence

*I yearn to see you
beyond my own projections.*

When I stop looking,
I start seeing.

~

Weeding the garden of the
mind is a dirty but rewarding
job.

~

Does this pleasure take you
away or bring you into the
moment?

Presence

In the absence of impatience, the fullness of the moment is realized.

～ᵉ～

I confess, I yearn for this moment to be different. It's a chronic condition.

～ᵉ～

If you don't have the energy to fully penetrate this moment, relax and let it have its way with you.

Each moment is like a twist on the kaleidoscope, offering magnificent designs except without symmetry.

YOU ARE HERE.
Even when there is a gap between where you are, and where you want to be, it's always good to have a starting point.

Presence

For a moment, I felt separated from God, frantically looking everywhere. Then I got present, and see that you've been there the whole time.

Relationship

Let's meet in that place where you are you, and I am me, yet we are more than we would be without the other.

I may adamantly insist that we do not belong to each other, but I'm equally certain that we belong together.

⌁

The best aphrodisiac for long-term relationships that have lost their spark is not new toys but heartfelt forgiveness.

⌁

The differences between us are not only the cause of our attraction, and a continual source of challenge, but that which complements us and makes our lives richer.

Relationship

The trick to cultivating conscious connection isto wake each other up — before the dream becomes a nightmare.

～

A complete custom remodel has been made in my heart to accommodate you.

～

Longing to be back in the honeymoon phase of a relationship is as unrealistic as wanting your maturing child to be nursing in your arms again.

There is no win, no accomplishment, no pleasure — when we are in right relationship — that could add to your life, but take away from mine.

~

One of the most beautiful gifts a loved one can give me is information on how to treat them better.

~

Humans have so much in common that relationships would be boring if it weren't for the constant game of denying our less desirable qualities, projecting them onto others, and judging them.

Relationship

Making love doesn't just happen between the sheets but when you stop what you're doing to greet your Beloved at the door, speak into the uncomfortable, call them for no reason, and thoughtfully put the toothpaste cap back on the tube.

Sacred Sex

If eyes are windows to the soul,
genitals must be the doorway.

I fancy foreplay that lasts for months, not minutes.

~

We pray before eating, why not before satisfying our other appetites?

~

The insatiable longing between my legs offers depth to my spiritual seeking.

Sacred Sex

A 'Sacred Slut' is not simply
someone who is having more
sex than you, but someone who,
like a God-drunk Sufi, is making
love to life, all of the time.

⁓

Sacred sex is a great way to
start the day, although, by
the time we get out of bed, it's
already evening.

⁓

Touching your body with the
lights out is like feeling my way
around an art museum
with a blindfold.

*In beholding your naked body,
I see that God's greatest
masterpiece is the human form,
genitals are her signature.*

~⁓

*My husband woke me up with a
huge reminder of who I am and
why I'm here. Thank God for
morning wood.*

Sacred Sex

Being a master lover isn't a function of knowing any particular moves, but a willingness to make them up as you go along.

~e~

I do not end where my skin begins, but I do enjoy exploring the heightened concentration of consciousness that meets me there.

~e~

Sex with someone you don't know is good, sex with someone you know is great, and sex with someone that is ultimately unknowable is God.

In Alchemy, fire is the agent of change, but the practitioner is warned never to let the flame get too hot. There is a parallel principle in sacred sexuality, thus the insistence on slow foreplay.

Sacred Sex

*At point of orgasm I'm filled
with a wordless whisper:
Give it to God!*

Sacrilege

Some might call me sacrilegious; but the way I see it, I'm just religious in the sack.

I will not worship false idols.
And I know they are false if
they are
too "holy" to fuck.

〜

I'm on my knees, what now?

〜

I am proud to be a part of
God's Harem. (It's not as sexist
as it sounds.)

Sacrilege

The aim of my religion is to prevent the devil from maintaining a monopoly on sex.

～

Western Non-dual Tantra for Dummies: God sucks and God blows.

～

My mattress has known more devotion than even the most highly-revered church pews.

A peak spiritual experience for me is hearing my atheist lover call out God's name at the height of his or her orgasm.

~

The wise priestess does not indulge in sex to compensate for the church's perverted repression, but restores prayer to its rightful place in sexual congress.

~

I'm not angry that the apes came in and pissed on the temple. They are, after all, apes. I am only upset that, in the moment, I didn't realize that even urine is sacred.

Sacrilege

I dreamt Jesus Christ was my lover. I anointed his feet with essential oils and dried them with my hair. Not so much in a devotional act — but because they were dirty!

The devil took one hard look at me, and put his tail between his legs.

I had a visitation from a benevolent presence; it looked like Jesus in flowing robes, with a wreath of thorns, except he was a she and had big tits. I was like: Is that you, Shesus?

I got more hate mail today.
The religious zealot writes:
"...and when you die, I hope
that God Almighty has his
way with you...."
And I'm thinking,
Me too.

Sacrilege

Hatha yoga is the practice of adjusting the body into particular positions so that, one might, for a moment, get a glimpse up God's skirt.

Sex

Sex is the fine art of making emptiness disappear.

*It's not about sex,
and it's all about sex.*

*The smartest way to kill sex
is to overthink it.*

*The best laid plans usually
involve plans to get laid.*

*Your words touch me deeper
than your hands, but not quite
as deep as your cock.*

Sex

*What if: When I'm tired ...
I sleep. When I'm hungry ...
I eat. And when I'm horny ...*

~

*Fingernails are fun for tickling
and scratching, but I prefer
short nails for penetration
purposes.*

~

*Sex without love is like eating
cake. It's delicious and
distracting for a short spell but
the satisfaction is
not sustaining.*

I'm committed to closing the gap between how awkwardly we fumble into each other in the flesh and how effortlessly we merge in my fantasies.

~

Your sex may be physically bigger and stronger than mine, but my sex takes great pleasure in containing yours.

Sex

Beyond all words and concepts, our bodies know how to further the conversation.

Sexual Healing

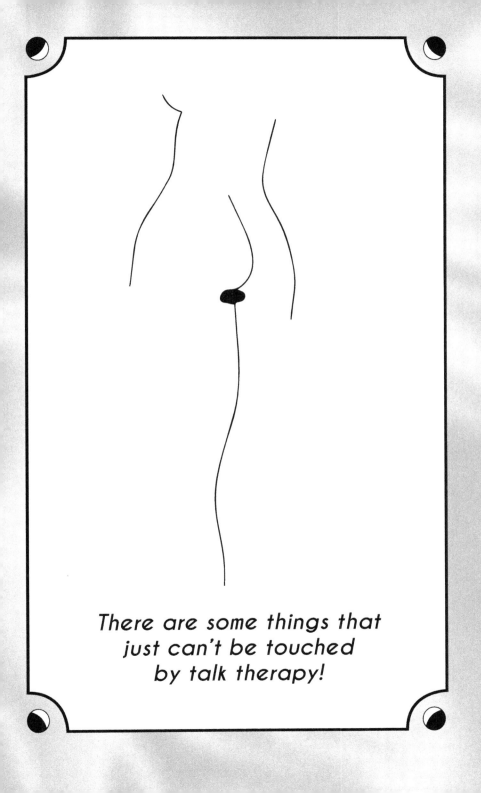

There are some things that just can't be touched by talk therapy!

Grab that which is unlovable and fiercely rape it with your love.

$\sim$

Confessions of a personal growth junkie: Therapy makes me horny.

$\sim$

Few things are more sensual than a man who knows how to wield a soft-on.

Sexual Healing

Sexual healers have the best job, they get to make women cum and grown men cry.

∿⌐

My self-esteem is great enough that I don't need a man to get an erection to feel sexy.

∿⌐

Sexual wholeness starts when we stop trying to stuff a square peg into a round hole.

I'm not attracted to a certain type or size of any particular body part, but those that embody the whole.

⁓

In my house having a headache, cramps or the blues is just an excuse to have more sex.

⁓

A healer may remedy or poison everyone they treat, and still be immune to their own medicine.

Sexual Healing

I'm honored when people give me permission to penetrate their deep psyche. Entering is painless, but I've learned to be careful when pulling out.

Shadow
Work

*Running from darkness is
exhausting and ineffective
compared to turning
on the light.*

The complaints I make about someone say more about me than they do about them — and the same can be said about the compliments.

∽

Many people "embrace" their shadow side, but how many people go all the way and make love to it?

∽

To the degree you are willing to hold my hand through the valleys, I'll be able to climb new peaks with you.

Shadow Work

The Beloved is even willing to show up as a hungry, lost and lonely seeker so that I can have the satisfaction of filling him with my devotion.

Dancing and fighting are the paradoxical energies within every system; you are that within me, and I am that within you.

On days when I don't listen to my dreams, they make themselves known in my waking life.

Shadow Work

We all have shadow qualities that we'd rather deny, ignore and lock behind an iron safe. By hiding them, we may temporarily protect ourselves and others from getting hurt, but keeping them in the dark is what eventually causes irreparable harm.

Shame

*I'm bidding farewell
to all shameful spaces
that deny the full spectrum
of my devotion.*

Shame on Shame.

⁓

*I confess, I'm shameless.
But guilt free and blameless,
because your erotic innocence
is so pure, not even I can
corrupt it.*

Shame

I'm ashamed, embarrassed, and afraid we'll be found out and crucified — but I never let my ego stop me.

～

I reject the idea that it's JUST sex ... as if there were a more revealing, dynamic, multi-dimensional form of communication. Sharing sexuality is like spontaneously downloading an elaborate new language that is completely unique to those involved ... that's all.

If you don't want to sell your soul to the devil, bare it often and freely, until it has no value to the wicked.

Shame

*Fucking is a rebellion.
Our bodies are an uprising of
pleasure against the systematic
shaming of — the source
of all human life.*

Separation

No matter how naked I strip,
there still seems to be
a veil between us.

God is the only one that gets me.

~

When the story of separation strikes, it's like a thunderstorm under my skin. Reality sails away like a kite and I struggle to reel it in by the string.

~

Despite how satisfying it is to feel right, it is an egoic story of separation.

Separation

"You're fired!" I say to the lawyer who runs around my mind collecting evidence of anything that is not love.

❧

I am always with you, yet simultaneously missing you.

❧

This wise oak has a wide network of branches and a vast root system, but is prone to over-identifying with one branch.

This craving to be met only becomes possible when I cease demanding it from one person and let the Universe see, hear, feel and get me.

～

Surrounded by darkness and separated by space, where do the stars get the courage to keep shining? When I feel alone, I look to the sky and this is what I wonder.

Separation

When I catch my mind stuck
in a self-loathing loop,
I stop and remember
I am a unique emanation of
the divine that usually trumps
all my human hallucinations.

Spirituality

Many spiritual folk give up praying, in favor of meditation — as if listening is somehow more important than talking. I prefer two-way conversations.

I hide behind my thoughts.

~

*At some point on stage —
every performer plays God. The
question is whether or not they
are acting.*

~

*From the perspective of
the Gods, all mountains are
molehills.*

Spirituality

May I root myself so deeply
in the divine that I am no
longer distracted by my outer
circumstance.

～

Every conversation
is a conversation with God.

～

If your God is judgmental,
jealous and damning — give
him a break — it sounds like he
may need a vacation.

Corruption is inevitable when the church's success depends on persuading people that they are not capable of a direct connection with the divine.

If our personalities weren't so damn distracting we might just find that we are essentially the same on the inside.

Dear God,
When I meet someone
who reminds me of you,
let me help them remember
who they are, by falling in love.

Spirituality

Our perception of reality can be utter awe, or that she is terrifying, depending entirely on whether we are seeing through the lense of love.

I step outside the temple in such oneness after worship, that amongst all the other seekers' shoes, I forget which ones are mine.

Ever had a spiritual hangover? Where God comes in while you're sleeping and rearranges the furniture so you wake up bumping into things in your own temple.

To lose sight of the divine, when you are as devotional as I am, can be blinding; but it's not nearly as bewildering as an atheist who starts to suspect that God existed behind his eyelids all along.

I used to have a "bat phone" to God, where I could dial her up with my urgent prayers. Gradually, I've been upgraded. Now, my direct line to God is like a high speed wireless intercom.

Spirituality

Remind me gently, please, that I'm delusional, anytime you catch me thinking that God's will is somehow separate from my own.

Tantra

There is a mountaintop where ascended masters hang out, laugh and make love. I used to think it was a myth or a metaphor, but in being with you, I know it's real.

*Your devotion arouses
my desire.*

~

*I am not a little bit tipsy but
downright God-drunk.*

~

*My non-dual directive is to
know Shiva and embody Shakti.*

Tantra

When Spirit takes form as the Beloved, it's only to serve as a doorway.

∽

There is a delicate art to seeing the Divine in the person before you. The amateur blindly projects their God concepts onto them while the adept simply sees the Beloved as they are.

∽

I'm writing the story of when Shakti meets Shiva, but this time, it's here and now.

When there is no false split between the sacred and profane, the temple can not be defiled.

∽

God may feel too immense and ubiquitous to grasp, but by holding you as my bindi, I melt into the infinite.

∽

Waking reality is extended worship. Every interaction is a puja station. Starting with solo practice in the shower, feeding the inner child breakfast, dancing with Shakti in the office, until meeting Shiva in the bedroom.

Tantra

*You have ruined me for others.
Ever since we started making
love, I can't help but see you in
the eyes of everyone.*

~⌒~

*My love is too free for this
fleshy frame, it flows in and out
of form, weaving an etheric
fabric between me and
the un-manifest.*

~⌒~

*They were married the moment
Shiva looked deeply into
Shakti's eyes and realized the
ocean is only blue because it
is reflecting the sky.*

*My non-dual directive
is to know Shiva
and embody Shakti.*

*This lucid dream is always
unfolding, even when I'm
awake, even when I'm unaware.*

Tantra

Why is it acceptable to drop to my knees in prayer, but other positions I use to worship the divine are not allowed in polite society?

Travel

I sat next to a Sufi on the
airplane who told me if I want
to get close to God, I must
get close to strangers.

As an American citizen, I live in a constant state of culture shock.

~

Leisure is the real secret weapon that most European countries have over America.

~

The walls around my heart are crumbling down — East Germany is having this affect on me.

Travel is a prescription to break bad habits, get perspective on our problems and turn the foreign into family.

∽

I spent a day at the museum in Figueres where Salavador Dali is entombed and I left thinking: "There is only one difference between a madman and me: I am not a man."

∽

In Germany I was told, "Tantra is pointless" — I'm sure something got lost in the translation.

In Paris men walk around swinging their baguettes so shamelessly by their hips, it's a wonder they don't get baguette envy.

The nude village in the south of France didn't allow photography. But I can't seem to erase the mental images I took of thousands of naked bodies splashing in the Mediterranean waters, with genitals of every color, shape, size, age and texture.

Goddess Pele put a spell on me. The land is alive. The trees are talking and bursting with medicinal fruit. Hawaii is lush, dirty, real. I am home.

Travel

Before my train pulls away from the platform he kisses me and says: "We may never see each other again, but we may never leave each other, either."

Truth

My desire for Truth is finally greater than my need for you to accept me.

Honesty is sexy.

I've always been a good storyteller, now the trick is becoming a truthteller.

Every belief is suspect. The more precious it is, the more interrogation it deserves.

Truth

To have ethics, you must have an awareness of who benefits and at whose expense.

〜

My devotion to Truth is all-consuming, it will eventually devour your distrust of me.

〜

Within this bundle of stimuli and response, there is a divine spark that catches in the presence of truth.

Telling the truth is the fastest
way to dissolve the distortion
between who you are, and who
you think you are.

⌒ℯ

Really? You are not speaking
the truth because you don't
want to hurt someone you
love? Or are you hurting
them by holding it back, and
underestimating them?

Truth

Truth is a turn on. I'm aroused by impeccability. Responsibility is irresistible. Considering consequences can be foreplay. And integrity makes me downright orgasmic!

Vulnerability

I would rather risk your horrified rejection by revealing myself fully than stay safely bundled in the arms of your uninformed acceptance.

How big is the gap between who you are alone versus who you are in public?

⁓

Love takes courage: when fear of loss looms big, we must open our hearts even bigger.

⁓

Love itself cannot cause harm. It's all the fucking barbwire we hang around the heart — to prevent loss — that hurts.

Vulnerability

It's easier for me to walk around physically naked than it is to strip off another layer of who I think I am.

⤳

I am no longer afraid of losing myself, for there is no part of me, that doesn't become more, by giving it to you.

⤳

I'm perplexed by human nature, particularly how we build defenses that push away the things we crave the deepest.

I'm retracting my claws and rolling over to show you my tender underbelly, not because you showed me yours ... but because, this is me.

~e

My head doesn't always want to drop my inhibitions, and melt the illusion of separation between us ... but my heart does.

~e

Feeling vulnerable — nothing to hide beneath — this is me: I act and say that which I feel and think, the moment it moves through me.

Vulnerability

Somewhere between our foolish hearts that are bloody from risking everything and the defensive walls that separate us — there is a field. I am stumbling around, trying to meet you there.

I thought you'd built a wall around your heart until I felt around a bit and discovered a doorknob.

Words

I may write the lyrics, but your
love puts them to music.

Your wordless depths make my passion eloquent.

⁓

Prayer is a special dialect between me and the divine, like baby-talk is for children or sweet talk for lovers.

⁓

I often find talking fruitless, but a few of your words have scattered like seeds in my heart and proliferated my soul.

Words

Penetrating conversation is the ultimate turn on. Our mouths and words are meant to stimulate, heal and pleasure each other.

I am a storyteller. The moral of the story is always about love. And I am constantly telling it; even when nobody is listening.

Your words are water. Not to quench a thirsty woman, but to make morning tea, to feed the organic garden, and to soak away the illusions of the mind. Thank you for showering me each day with the fountain of your soul.

Words

*What good are words in the
company of your beauty?
I'd be better off trying
to describe silence.*

Work

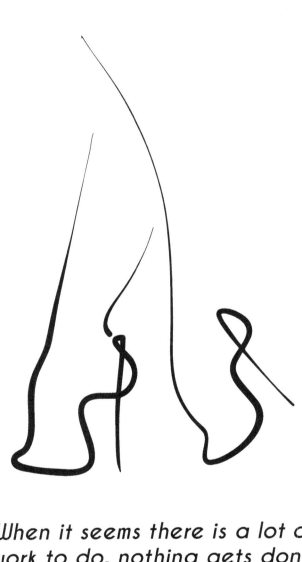

When it seems there is a lot of
work to do, nothing gets done.
Then I remember it is all play,
and I become unstoppable.

When a stranger asks me what I do, I say: love. Because in fact, that's what I do.

~e

Those of us who are on the planet to teach love, must first contend with the fear that comes up for the healing.

Work

If your vocation doesn't turn you on, change it. The same could be said about relationship, home, hobbies or even religion.

⌇⌇⌇

There is an essential distinction between a career and a calling. Don't let the demands of your bills, your boss or even your clients, distract you from your real work.

When surrender feels too steep,
I set my intention on service
and it all seems to work out.

Work

I woke up and realized I am a miracle worker, as is anybody who works with humans.

Writing

It is impossible to describe
God in words, but a writer is
not burdened
by what's possible.

A writer must live off the page if they ever intend to come alive on it.

～

I have a fetish for the inner workings of the introvert; they tend to be people whose inner world is more interesting than the outer.

～

An elaborate web of perverted fantasies hangs over my head like a dreamcatcher when I write.

Writing

The most enlightened poetry
arises out of self pleasure;
'tis a pity my hands are too
engaged to wield a pen.

⁓

There is symbolism in
everything: this tea, this pillow,
this kiss on your mouth. It is
what it is, yet it is more than
it seems.

⁓

The writer's burden is to select
the perfect series of words
while knowing such symbols
only squish the juice out of the
human experience.

A new idea is like a seed embedded in edible flesh. There is so much pleasure in sharing the outer sweetness, but actually planting and parenting it takes work.

~e

I don't consider myself an intellectual, but I can bullshit with the best of them.

~e

Writers block is an indication that you are attached to quality. If you give yourself permission to produce quantity, without clinging to concepts of 'good' or 'bad,' everything flows.

Writing

I'm supposed to be editing my script, but ended up making love all day. It's funny how some forms of procrastination are easier to forgive than others.

A good book un-writes our destiny.

Acknowledgements

ART:
Deep bow to the brilliant, kinky, zen, erotic artist: François Dubeau.
Stumbling onto your art somehow quiets my existential suffering and
helps me make sense of the world.

MY FAMILY:
Gratitude to Michael, the love of my life. And my son, Devin Echo
McClure, who inspires me daily with the wit and wisdom of a nine-
year-old ninja.

I'm filled with devotion for my muse, girlfriend and Bitch, Roxanne
DePalma. Warm waves of gratitude to both her and her husband.
Daniel is a Big-Picture visionary whose genius speaks to me like
Shams. Together these two have made the greatest contribution to my
love life, inspiring me towards ever-emerging new possibilities.

Praise to the women in my bloodline: The goddess who brought me
into this world, Rosa Espinoza. My step mom Laurie who's shown me
what it means to be a woman on a Mission. Mamma Terry, age 96,
who is still making love to life. And gratitude to my late Tia Elvira,
and Mi Abuelita Ester. RIP.

SUPERPOD:
Although this may seem like a simple list of names, it is an
invocation to the individuals who've indelibly touched my heart, for
each time I meet with one of my lovers, an entire Universe is created.
Thank you: Cheri Reeder. Stacy Lynn. Jennifer Gold. Jesse Norton.
Tahl Gruer. Tziporah Kingsbury. Viraja Prema. Adam Paulman.
James Schmachtenberger. Sharmila Graefer. Lalita Alaya. Summer
Athena Fah. Megan Ferry. Kevin Dalfonzo. Sonia Reece. David Steel.
Sarah Jane. Janos Tisza Novak. Julie Kondor. Cathleene Cienfuegos
and enormous gratitude to Rachel Rickards.

I'm also in awe of my long distance lovers who've traveled through time and space and keep stretching my love: Baba Dez. Reid Mihalko. Charles & Christy Muir. Laughing Hawk. Ohad Ezrahi. Dawn Cherie. Diana Adams. Friar Tuck. Jonathan Robinson. Kirsten Young. Tracy Elise. Sarasvati Ting. Bruce Cooley, Dave Donatiu. Talyaa Liera. La'akea Family. Cain Carroll. Sanjiv Sidhu. Sammy Bliss & my first girlfriend: Rayna McInturf.

CONTENT READERS:
Annie Sprinkle PhD (who inspired the title of this book), Beth Stevens PhD, Jill Nagel and Tim Fullerton. Special thanks to the artistry of my father for influencing my poetry, inspiring me to appreciate line drawings and suggesting that I break the sutras into several volumes.

COPY EDITING & PUBLISHING:
Mary VanMeer, a reliable virtual book goddess! Her fierce attention to details frees me up so that I can focus on hearing my soul sing through me.

INTERIOR DESIGN:
DJ Rogers for her brilliant and insightful designs. She has a knack for weaving multiple contradictory ideas into a fun, efficient and seamless collaboration.

GRAPHIC DESIGN:
Miguel Kagan for volunteering his vision and consulting hours as a labor of love. I would not be a published author without him.

PHOTOGRAPHY:
Inside Photo of Kamala Devi: Julie Kondor, www.KondorImaging.com. Back Cover: Top Photo: J. Buttaz, a renaissance man in the audio and visual arts. Bottom Photo: By François Dubeau's talented and brilliant wife Sophie Trudeau.

MY READERS:
I have no way of knowing who will be magnetized to this body of work, or how it will change our lives, but in the ground of my being, I trust that an evolutionary transformation will come from our co-creation.

About The Artist

François Dubeau's work is a delightful paradox. Combining traditional techniques with the most modern of digital tools, Dubeau explores the simplest form of expression. His artistic exploration is one of simplicity, striving for the elemental.

Dubeau's work proceeds from a rejection of the growing complexity and rapidly accelerating pace of our modern lives. Going back to the most instinctual of basics, Dubeau's work suggests a "modern cave painting," exploring themes and forms that have inhabited humankind's psyche since the dawn of time. His work is a soothing antidote to the stress, hysteria and flashing lights of the outside world.

Combining the traditional techniques of the engraver, of the illustrator and of the painter, Dubeau's work is as timeless as it is thoroughly modern. Using a digital stylus, Dubeau explores raw, boundless movement on his virtual canvas, a random gesture always serving as the starting point. A single line often translates into hours of work as a stroke is forever repeated — never twice the same way — until the artist is satisfied with the end result. Once a drawing is complete, it is transferred to paper or canvas. For his canvas work, Dubeau picks up traditional paints and brushes to create unique free-flowing pieces with exceptional depth and movement.

Dubeau's mastery of digital tools as a creative medium gives him complete freedom over his work. His combining of traditional and modern techniques allows him to bridge past and present, authenticity and simplicity in a truly unique, original way.

http://www.francoisdubeau.com/

About The Author

Kamala Devi is a bisexual Latin woman of Jewish descent who was raised between conservative Orange County and a ranch in Mexico. Throughout college, she produced a handful of feminist-themed plays and was a gay and lesbian activist. She founded the first bisexual and lesbian women's discussion group at her university.

Before she even heard the word polyamory, her college girlfriend pointed out that she was in love with a male yoga teacher and she began dating them both... After graduation, she moved to a drumming commune in Hawaii where she directed the lesbian, gay, transgender and bisexual Pride festival of Honolulu in 1997. She met a professional dominatrix who introduced her to the world of kink.

After a spontaneous sexual awakening on the islands, she began backpacking and studying yoga throughout Europe, Southeast Asia, and China. When she returned to California, she met her life partner, Michael, at a Tantric puja in San Diego.

Together they took a pilgrimage to South India to study Goddess worship from a guru who channels Kali. The 2004 Sumatran Tsunami struck the very beaches where they were at the exact moment their airplane lifted off. This event inspired Kamala Devi's first novel, *Don't Drink the Punch: An Adventure in Tantra*.

When pregnant, they bought a beach house that Michael converted into an eco-friendly temple where they home-birthed their son Devin Echo McClure. He is now an 8 year old bilingual scientist who loves to sail and surf. Devin is proud to be raised in a polyamorous family with a variety of live-in lovers who were featured on Showtime's docu-series, *Polyamory: Married & Dating* which ran for 2 seasons.

Kamala Devi's girlfriend Roxanne is co-author of the erotic novel, *52 Fridays with My Bitch*. Together, they are part of a circle of about a dozen lovers who are transparent about everything, this group is affectionately called the "Superpod."

Kamala Devi is the founder of both TantraPalooza and PolyPalooza, which are annual festivals for free lovers. She also created and directs Tantra Theater, a collective of artists, teachers and healers who offer live performance art to heal sexual guilt and shame. www.TantraTheater.TV

She is co-author of *Sacred Sexual Healing* with Baba Dez and is featured in his award-winning documentary, *Sex Magic*. She is on faculty with International School of Temple Arts. She has made several instructional DVDs including *Earning your BLACKBELT in Relationship* with Reid Mihalko.

Today, Kamala Devi is a highly-visible spokesperson and has facilitated over a thousand sex-positive events in the last 20 years. Kamala Devi has also appeared on the *Tyra Banks Show*, *Discovery Channel*, *Morning Show Live*, *Inside Edition*, and MTV's *True Life*, to name a few. Her future vision is to create a retreat center so people from all over the world can liberate their love lives. Kamala Devi is devoted to helping people liberate love and ethically awaken their sexuality, because she feels it is necessary for the evolution of the planet. She is especially interested in training healers, teachers and visionaries so they can become Love Leaders around the world.

Kamala Devi takes pleasure in nature, massage, vegan foods, snuggling, dance, theater and performance art. Her ultimate turn-on is penetrating conversation. Kamala Devi is a natural muse and uses her body as a doorway to enlightenment. She knows how to use her mouth and words to stimulate and heal people. She is also a deep listener, and loves silence, touch and laughter. For free resources on how to become a better lover go to: KamalaDevi.com

Want More?

Additional Copies:

To order additional copies of *Sacred Slut Sutras* securely online, please visit www.KamalaDevi.com.

More by Kamala Devi:

Polyamory Pearls: Radical Wisdom on Open relationships, Jealousy, Group Sex, and other Spiritual Pursuits Vol. 2
Don't Drink the Punch: An Adventure in Tantra
Sacred Sexual Healing: The SHAMAN Method of Sex Magic
with Baba Dez Nichols
The Polyamory Roadmap (Ebook)
Earning you BLACKBELT in Relationship (DVD) with Reid Mihalko
The Pleasure Bible with Marc Gafni
52 Fridays with My Bitch with Roxanne DePalma
The Sacred Slut, A One-Woman Show and other Performances by Kamala Devi are available online at: www.TantraTheater.TV

More by François Dubeau:

Prints, Limited Editions and Originals all Lovingly Produced by the Artist at www.francoisdubeau.com or contact him at francois@francoisdubeau.com

Public Appearances:

Kamala Devi is available for speaking engagements and select private healing sessions. To inquire about our availability and services please visit KamalaDevi.com or send an email to info @KamalaDevi.com

ZENDOW PRESS

Printed in Great Britain
by Amazon

39801142R00155